ideals®
EASTER

W9-AXL-548

As God sends spring at winter's end and birds
return to build again—as dark woods quicken into
green beneath the kiss of April's rain, so shall I
wake one happy day and feel the pulse of life anew,
looking out with fearless eyes towards a broader,
brighter view—discovering forgotten dreams and
happiness so long denied—learning how to live
again, by many sorrows purified. As new sap rises
in the bough and bursts the folded buds apart, so
will hope bring forth her flowers and joy return
unto my heart.

Patience Strong

ISBN 0-8249-1009-5 350

IDEALS—Vol. 39, No. 2 February MCMLXXXII IDEALS (ISSN 0019-137X) is published eight times a year,
January, February, April, June, July, September, October, November
by IDEALS PUBLISHING CORPORATION, 11315 Watertown Plank Road, Milwaukee, Wis. 53226
Second class postage paid at Milwaukee, Wisconsin. Copyright © MCMLXXXII by IDEALS PUBLISHING CORPORATION.
POSTMASTER: Send address changes to Ideals, Post Office Box 2100, Milwaukee, Wis. 53201
All rights reserved. Title IDEALS registered U.S. Patent Office.
Published simultaneously in Canada.

ONE YEAR SUBSCRIPTION—eight consecutive issues as published—$15.95
TWO YEAR SUBSCRIPTION—sixteen consecutive issues as published—$27.95
SINGLE ISSUE—$3.50

Publisher, James A. Kuse
Editor/Ideals, Colleen Callahan Gonring
Associate Editor, Linda Robinson
Production Manager, Mark Brunner
Photographic Editor, Gerald Koser
Copy Editor, Barbara Nevid
Art Editor, Duane Weaver

The Edge of Spring

I roam the timely countryside
and touch the edge of spring;
I feel the breath of angels
like flowers whispering.

I nudge the shape of shadows
that soothe the morning sun;
I brush the scent of blossoms
on the petals having none.

I flirt with one-eyed daisies
that wave with daring grace;
I watch the morning glories
lift their smiling face.

I reach for time eternal
that somehow molds a tree;
I grasp a climbing rainbow,
and colors encompass me.

I portray a humble figure
amidst this work of art;
I framed this bit of heaven
and hung it in my heart.

Wayne B. Dayton

The Break

The close observer of nature notes her signs with keen awareness, as each one makes its advent into a world that is apparently always ready for it. He watches the sky and landscape, detecting changes almost before they occur. If there is a phenomenon, he is first to behold it, for his senses are tuned to the sights and sounds of the universe.

I am strangely captivated by that brief hiatus between the seasons when an air of expectancy prevails. It is a quiet spell when the landscape lies ready to assume an entirely new character. Time pauses at the bend, looks back, then plunges madly ahead. When the world is on the threshold of spring, its harbingers multiply daily, and there is surprise after surprise.

It is heartening to awaken early in a morning in the break between winter and spring and hear a flock of wild geese chattering in the sky. I rush outside to catch a glimpse of them moving northward across the heavens, heralding the return of brighter days, and marvel at the orderliness of their flight. As surely as there is sunrise and sunset, there is a Power that directs from behind the scene, and they soon will find rest among their fellows in the sanctuary of their destination.

It is on one of spring's vibrant days that I look with expectation to a trip in the country to view the handiwork of nature in the hills, valleys and pasturelands. There is nothing to hinder the whole of nature on the move. What one sees is not a showy facade but a complete transformation, and the entire scene stands in testimony to the fact that summer and winter, seedtime and harvest shall not cease as long as the earth remains. The incessant croaking of frogs in farm ponds, where the last bit of ice has just melted, and the faraway call of the whippoorwill in early evening are certain signs that winter is on the wane. Nature rubs her sleepy eyes in preparation for an abrupt awakening.

Surely, as man views this changing panorama, he is bound to know that wonders never cease, and springtime is graphic evidence of this fact. It is the supernatural revealed in nature. It is miracle after miracle. It is a foretaste of resurrection glory, and he who observes this spectacular transcendency sees in it a phenomenon.

Sarah Alice Burns

Easter

Awake, you million tiny mites!
You've slept through winter's frigid nights.
Now spring has come. It's come to stay,
I know; I heard the bluebird say,
    "Awake."

Awake, you countless buds and flowers!
Your time has come. You've waited hours.
Now throw your fragrance on the air.
Your tender shoots are fresh and fair.
    Awake!

Awake, all men, to spring's new life!
All you, who hold to selfish strife,
Let Easter blessings on you fall;
Hark to the Resurrection call.
    Awake!

Leon Eugene Wright

The Angel, Spring

She creeps in like a thief at night,
Awakens the buds, sends the birds to flight,
Melts the winter ice and snow,
Bids them to little streamlets go,
Pearls each dewy blade of grass,
Gentles the breezes as they pass,
Whispers "Arise" to each wee thing.
An array of colors she doth bring,
Stirs the farmer to his plow,
The leaf on every sleepy bough,
Tunes all nature's voice to song,
Makes each new day a little more long,
Glorifies the coming of Eastertide,
Heralds her way both far and wide,
Sends warm sunshine, April showers,
Directs the daffodil's dance of flowers.
All hail the handmaiden of the king,
The welcome angel, Spring.

Ruby Davenport Kish

Spring Message

There is a message to the heart in every greening bough,
In each embryonic sheaf yet closely furled,
The patterns made by newly breaking sod,
Birdsong across a morning freshly pearled,
In air heavy and sweet with long awaited rain,
Hillsides, barren, once again now brightly spilled;
Oh, the world itself is glory to His name
And richly blessed with promises fulfilled!

Mona K. Guldswog

Springtime on the Farm

Spring is on the hillside.
Spring is everywhere,
In the hills and valleys,
Even in the air,

Hyacinths and tulips
Pushing with their might,
Breaking out of prison,
Seeking for the light.

Happy birds are building,
With a merry song,
Nests to house their babies
When the days are long.

Life itself is stirring
With its radiant charm.
Oh, what is half so wonderful
As springtime on the farm!

Eunice Elmore Heizer

An abandoned homestead borders on my property, but I do not consider the dilapidated buildings an eyesore nor the gnarled orchard haunted during a full moon. Instead, I welcome the old place as my most interesting neighbor.

In early spring I go, empty basket swinging, to borrow from my neighbor. Cutting thick, succulent spears from the asparagus bed still flourishing beside the barn, I learn to respect the wisdom of the gardener who established these roots in such a fertile base. Unlike his transient successors, this person planned to spend his lifetime with the land. Beyond the house, a strawberry patch—growing wild now—yields perfectly rounded berries possessing a flavorful tartness unique from their hybrid heirs. Adjoining the strawberry patch, a thriving clump of raspberry bushes promises quarts of berries to the patient scavenger.

Vegetables, fruit, and nectar for my bees flourish on this land. I realize that I could collect a living here. Walking home across the spacious fields, I experience a thrill akin to that of those who first settled here. A special independence is born of providing for my needs directly from the land.

Commenting on man's relationship to the land, the respected naturalist, Joseph Wood Krutch, said, "If we do not permit the earth to produce beauty and joy, it will in the end not produce food either."

Surely these homesteaders understood that truth. Pungent cinnamon roses, old-fashioned lilacs, and sweet peas gone wild outline the crumbling fieldstone foundation of the farmhouse. More than the

My Favorite Neighbor

orchard or the cleared fields, these blossoms remind me of the people who shared their lives with this farm. Alone now, the land continues to acknowledge the care of its first guardians.

And I, an intruder upon this relationship, absorb a bit of its loveliness, for I have learned many things while visiting my neighbor. With my neighbor's guidance I have learned to listen for the melody of breezes playing upon the great white pine and to watch for patterns in a spider's web. I have also learned to welcome solitude because I realize that loneliness need not be connected with being alone.

Inspired by the example of my venerable neighbor, I have filled the sterile greenery of my lawn with bulbs and shrubs and fruit trees. They grow in twisting patterns, spring up in unexpected places, and continuously entice me with their changes.

But they also lend a permanence previously lacking in my hurried existence. As I bury a seedling's spindly roots or toss fine seed against the soil, I bond my life to the land. For my neighbor has taught me to value permanence and has shown me legacies the land extends to those who care.

Kathleen S. Abrams

Buds of Beauty

For every aspiration of the heart,
God has made a living, vital counterpart
In buds of beauty, fragrance, color, form;
And each glad spring these blossoms are reborn.

As long as God sends forth His graceful flowers,
Man's heart can hold no dismal, haunted hours.
They are His breath, a loving benediction,
Blessing the soul's sweet search for recognition.

Mabelle A. Lyon

The Metamorphosis of Spring

Spring's mystical womb
Delivers new bloom
Each year;
With bud and perfume
She flees Winter's tomb.
With cheer

And heeding the call
To be Summer's thrall,
She leaps
To spread her green shawl
In emerald sprawl,
Then creeps

Inside Autumn's gown
With burnished gold crown
And reigns
In orange-red-brown.
But soon tumbling down,
She wanes,

As Winter winds blow
To end her grand show
And hide
Her last bit of glow
Beneath pall of snow.
Spring sighed,
Then laughed from below,
"Oh, new embryo,
Abide."

Sandra M. Haight

Springtime in the Desert

This is the desert's one triumphant hour;
A western basin, shunned in summer's heat
And winter's desolate cold, has come to flower
With beauty that compels the wariest feet.

Miraculous is the exquisite, brief bloom
Of this harsh land—the rosy creeping phlox,
Blue harebell, yucca's soft, white plume,
The lichen's gold embroidery on rocks.

No manmade garden ever knew such size
Or graced its soil with such a blossom-maze—
A lupine-sea that ends where mountains rise,
A field of paintbrush like a prairie blaze!

Sudie Stuart Hager

Easter Thoughts

Easter thoughts are wondrous thoughts,
When human hearts are blessed
With knowledge that the barren world
Was but asleep, at rest.

Easter thoughts are wondrous thoughts
Of life anew and spring
And all the joyful certainty
A flowering world can bring.

Ideals' Best-Loved Poets

Virginia Blanck Moore

Virginia Blanck Moore is a familiar name to *Ideals* readers. A Phi Beta Kappa graduate of the University of Iowa, she earned her degree in journalism. She married Robert Moore who was a counselor for the Iowa Commission for the Blind. Virginia Moore's book, *Seeing Eye Wife,* describes her married life. Her first poems to be published appeared in *Better Homes and Gardens* when she was only a freshman in college. In 1954 she began writing for *Ideals* after a friend sent her a copy of the magazine as a Christmas gift. Until her recent retirement, Mrs. Moore had been Information Services Coordinator for Iowa Children's and Family Services, a state-wide, non-governmental agency. She has been the editor-in-chief of the Iowa Poetry Association since 1975 while continuing to write her special style of inspirational poetry for others to enjoy.

Spring's Return

Sweet is the smell of lilacs;
Soft is the sound of rain;
Silver the color of droplets
A-splash on the windowpane.
Cool are the April breezes
Blowing across my brow;
Velvet the pussy willows
Climbing their slender bough;
Silky the new grass growing
Close to the open door;
Thankful the hearts of mankind
That spring has returned once more.

Springtime

It's jumping rope and marble time
Among the lads and lasses,
And time when far-off vacant stares
Meet teachers in their classes.

For how can thoughts be anchored down
To spelling, brought to bear
On such things as arithmetic
When spring is in the air?

No scolding words can make a child
Work like the well-known beaver
When he, like me, is suffering from
A bad case of spring fever!

March

March is winter saying good-bye
And reluctant still to go.
March is spring coming over the hill
With a shy but warm "Hello."

Walk Softly

Walk softly on a woodland path;
Put each foot down with care,
For those who own this bit of world
Are round us everywhere.

Walk gently on a woodland path,
For trespassers are we
On land that's owned by furry ones—
Bird, butterfly and bee.

Drink in the beauty as we go
Among the emerald bowers,
But softly tread and gently step;
This sylvan spot's not ours.

Spring Portents

Snow may linger in the corners
Of a sheltered nook;
Ice may fringe the shaded places
On the banks of pond and brook.

Cold may be the wind that's blowing,
Pale the sunshine, gray the sky,
But winter-weary mankind's certain
Spring is drawing very nigh.

For someone found a willow branch
Trimmed with furry gray;
Someone saw green sprouts thrust upward
Where snow lay yesterday.

Someone saw a robin redbreast;
Someone heard him sing—
Welcome signs and certain portents
When the winter turns to spring.

Easter and Spring

Easter and springtime!
How lovely to know
The sun and the showers
Have bid the grass grow.

How lovely to feel
The sweet warmth of the air
And see budlets burst
Into bloom everywhere.

How lovely to listen
As feathered friends sing
To bring us the message,
"It's Easter and spring!"

Spring's Charm

The feel of spring is in the rain
That trickles down my windowpane
And brings a freshness to the air
As wind blows softly on my hair.

The sight of spring is in the leaves
Of tulips growing neath the eaves
And holding buds that soon will bloom
Where hyacinths will give them room.

The charm of spring is for the eyes
That watch new growth from bare limbs rise
And for the ears that clearly hear
The welcome sounds with notes of cheer.

Eunice Mackinson

Golden Trumpets

Golden trumpets in bright clusters,
  Tossing gently in the breeze,
Waken us to springtime's dawn
  Like revelry at daybreak's ease.

Heralds of the morn of seasons,
  First arrivals on the scene,
Rousing Earth from barren slumber
  And the still of winter's dream,

Riotous in all their splendor,
  Joining nature's symphony,
They resound in jubilation,
  Such a welcomed melody.

Michele Arrieh

March Winds

March winds are blowing a welcome to spring;
Birds flying northward merrily sing,
"Winter is ended; the sun and the rain
Are bringing the grass and the flowers again."

Hark to the wind's song, March on the hill
Calling all wildflowers their promise fulfill.
Winds through the garden, where bulbs
   have been sleeping,
Find quite a few that are eagerly peeping.

Hear the winds cry as they rush past,
"The glory of springtime is coming at last."
They foretell the gifts summer will yield—
Flowers in the garden, grain in the field.

                    Essie L. Mariner

Birds in Spring

I knew 'twas geese,
There in the sky,
Before I heard their
Familiar cry,
For far overhead
I could see
The perfect formation
Of a V—
A sure sign that
Winter's passed
And spring has come
Again, at last.
Then perched on the feeder
Full of seed,
A pair of blue jays
Come to feed.
The robins, with their
Bright red breast,
Are working hard to build
Their nest.
It's nice to know
When you hear them sing,
They've brought the promise
Of summer and an early spring.

Florence Weber

Fragrance

God gives us many perfect gifts
Of sight and touch and smell
And many other lovely things
Too numerous to tell,
But what a strange, exquisite thing
Is this mysterious power
To draw within ourselves
The very spirit of a flower.

And as I sit here in my room
So quiet and so still,
I catch the drifting fragrance of
A golden daffodil.
I breathe the inner soul of it;
It yields itself to me.
I tremble on the threshold of
This hidden mystery.

It tells me spring is on its way
In spite of rain and cold.
It whispers of the budding trees
And days of green and gold.
And I can face the hours of waiting,
Patient and serene,
Content with this sweet message
From the world of the unseen.

Patience Strong

Harbinger of Spring

Joan C. Callahan

Gentle lamb, so small, so meek,
What thoughts have you
Of this greening world neath brilliant skies,
So new to your awakened eyes,
Where you frolic on unsteady feet.

Gone now winter's gloom and cold, and graying snows
Have melted into lazy streams
Where you pause with puzzled stare
To contemplate reflections there.

Gentle lamb, will you flee in sudden fright
At sounds so strange, so loud—
A buzzing bee, a scolding bird, or
Rumblings from the lowering clouds?

And will the honeyed breeze
In sweet enticement
Lure your curious nose
To find excitement
In the upturned flower, the warming sun,
Flickering shadows on newborn grass.

Enjoy, enjoy, my little lamb, these carefree days;
From nature's cup take pleasure;
For in this, the springtime of your life,
Pure joys abound in endless measure.

And when the hour was come, he sat down, and the twelve apostles with him. And he said unto them, With desire I have desired to eat this passover with you before I suffer: For I say unto you, I will not any more eat thereof, until it be fulfilled in the kingdom of God. And he took the cup, and gave thanks, and said, Take this, and divide it among yourselves: For I say unto you, I will not drink of the fruit of the vine, until the kingdom of God shall come.

And he took bread, and gave thanks, and brake it, and gave unto them, saying, This is my body which is given for you: this do in remembrance of me. Likewise also the cup after supper, saying, This cup is the new testament in my blood, which is shed for you.

Luke 22:14-20

MAUNDY THURSDAY

The last meal which He ate with them,
The night before He died,
Was one which they would oft recall
When He was crucified.

He talked with them and washed their feet;
He gave them bread and wine,
That in remembrance they might do
The act which was divine.

"No servant greater than his Lord,"
"No love so great as this"—
The words of life preceding death
Betrayed by friendship's kiss.

So silver from Iscariot's hand
Has tinkled down the years;
Man's greed has hanged his guilty self
And drowned his deeds in tears.

Alice Kennelly Roberts

Then delivered he him therefore unto them to be crucified. And they took Jesus, and led him away. And he bearing his cross went forth into a place called the place of a skull, which is called in the Hebrew Golgotha: Where they crucified him, and two others with him, on either side one, and Jesus in the midst.

And Pilate wrote a title, and put it on the cross. And the writing was JESUS OF NAZARETH THE KING OF THE JEWS.

John 19:16-19

GOOD FRIDAY

My Savior climbed Golgotha's hill,
Bearing His heavy load.
As painfully He upward toiled
Along that uphill road,
Great drops of sweat and drops of blood
Dripped for a cause sublime.
The cross He bore, the thorns He wore
Were His; the sins were mine!

They nailed Him to the cross of pain,
And there He died to win
The evil, stubborn hearts of men
And save them from their sin.
He laid His life, a bridge across,
Whereon we all may pass
Unto the Father's loving arms
To be redeemed at last.

M. Mae Fisher

And when she had thus said, she turned herself back, and saw Jesus standing, and knew not that it was Jesus. Jesus saith unto her, Woman, why weepest thou? whom seekest thou? She, supposing him to be the gardener, said unto him, Sir, if thou have borne him hence, tell me where thou has laid him, and I will take him away. Jesus saith unto her, Mary. She turned herself, and saith unto him, Rabboni; which is to say, Master. Jesus saith unto her, Touch me not; for I am not yet ascended to my Father: but go to my brethren and say unto them, I ascend unto my Father, and your Father; and to my God, and your God. Mary Magdalene came and told the disciples that she had seen the Lord, and that he had spoken these things unto her.

John 20:14-18

Easter Morning

A cross against a pale gray sky,
His grieving people huddled by,
The Master's body quiet, torn,
Wearing still the crown of thorns,
Loving hands took Him down,
Wrapping Him in linens white,
Placed Him in the waiting tomb
And kept their vigil through the night.
Three days passed while they did mourn.
Then He arose! New hope was born
From out the dark and flowered tomb,
Assuaging mankind's anguished doom.
The sun rose high that misty morn
On the first of Easters, newly born.

Mary Frances Watkins

The Easter Symbol

It was the ending of a time and the beginning of a time. It was the darkness, and it was the light. It was tears, and it was hope. It was the crucifixion of Christ.

The sky was dark with hatred and prejudice, and mankind seemed to be upon the darkest hour.

Thunder rolled across the sky, and lightning sliced crazily through the somber clouds.

Some men rejoiced, others wept, and in the mortal sense all men were at a loss.

The forest was alive with beasts, their senses tuned to something far beyond their realm of understanding. They could smell the shame and error in the air.

The beasts converged upon the meadow. Once a grazing spot of tranquillity, it now embraced the darkness. The rumbling of the sky was warning menacingly of a change. They crowded close, each a part of nature's scene. From field mouse to mountain lion, the herds began to grow in number. They communicated silently, the confusion and the fear always present in their eyes.

Soon it was decided. They must discover why the sky was angry. Could they be to blame for the holocaust upon the hill? They must send a courier. They would solve the mystery for themselves, but they must send him soon. They must know the reason for all the anger in the sky.

The meadow swiftly filled to its capacity with all God's creatures, and they began to choose. What beast could complete this task? He should not be too large for fear of discovery nor too small to comprehend everything. He must be fleet of foot and have a coat that would conceal his presence among the rocks and trees.

A judgment was reached. It was decided that the rabbit would complete the journey. His brown coat would not attract notice, and his speed would bring the answer quickly.

The rabbit set about his mission with the speed granted to him by his creator. Through the forest, over streams, and down the hills through the heavy air he raced. His nostrils twitched with apprehension. Then, he saw it in the distance, but what were those giant trees? They had no leaves and only one branch across the top. He sped closer; he must get a better look. The scent of death and evil pervaded his senses. He did not like the smell. It was the smell of man, a scent he had grown to fear.

He traveled faster now, he could observe three trees in the distance, but men were a part of those trees. He was confused; his wonder was intense. He saw men laughing, women grieving; he saw the sky turn blacker as the thunder attained its peak.

He reached the base of the strange trees and crouched beneath the bush closest to the middle tree. He gazed upward; there was a gentleness and a sadness in the man's eyes. He did not fear this man. He knew He would cause no harm. He felt the wrong. He knew that mankind had erred, but he could not help. He glanced up again; it may have been because of an instinct or an inner sense granted to all God's creatures that he knew this special man meant peace and love for all.

He remained motionless; his eyes returned again to the gentle man's gaze, and slowly his fur began to lighten from brown to gray to white until it was as pure as snow. This was the sign—he knew it was! Man and beast alike could still have hope. He paused once more in wonder to look at the face. The eyes could almost speak; the rabbit understood the silent message. It was all too clear, a reminder of man's ignorance and helplessness, and the rabbit would be that reminder throughout all the centuries to come. He would be the special sign; he would represent this day.

He began his journey back to the meadow and the anxious beasts. They must know what he knew. His coat was now a winter white—this would be the symbol and the proof that man and beast alike would share this day forever.

Stephanie Williams Hope

Resurrection Day

The dazzling rays of light today
Disperse the cold and gloom.
The shortening shadows seem to say,
"Come forth ye from the tomb.
This is your resurrection day;
Let springtime flowers bloom.
The birds shall sing their songs, so gay;
All nature shall resume
Her healing growth from earthy clay
And scatter sweet perfume."

Leon Eugene Wright

Easter Tapestry
&
Special Thoughts about Springtime

Pussy Willows

More soft than press of baby lips
They fleck the russet willow-slips
Before the bluebirds hither wing—
These first, faint footfalls of the spring.

Arthur Guiterman

A Prayer for You at Easter

May the blessed Easter story
Of the Resurrection bring
New hopes, new peace,
New joy and love,
And make your heart to sing—

"HE IS RISEN!"

Pearl McKinney

March

Windy days and roller skates,
Boys with kites and hiking dates,
Lawns fresh-combed and washed with rain,
Boisterous March is here again.

Margaret Williams Stevens

Spring

March comes in
on roller skates.
It brings skinned knees,
wind-tossed trees,
puddles, giggles,
and spring.

Lee Crews

Spring tiptoed through a rainbow
When she came in today;
She only stayed a moment
To blow the clouds away.

June Masters Bacher

Easter Joys

May the Easter sunrise
Chase every cloud away,
Bringing many blessings
And joys to fill your day.

Pearl McKinney

Sweet Peas

Here are sweet peas, on tiptoe for a flight,
With wings of gentle flush o'er delicate white
And taper fingers catching at all things
To bind them all about with tiny rings.

John Keats

Come, gentle spring, ethereal mildness, come;
And from the bosom of yon dropping cloud,
While music wakes around, veiled in a shower
Of shadowing roses, on our plains descend.

James Thomson

Spring hangs her infant blossoms on the trees,
rocked in the cradle of the western breeze.

William Cowper

Violet

A violet by a mossy stone,
Half hidden from the eye,
Fair as a star when only one
Is shining in the sky.

William Wordsworth

Field Abloom

A field abloom with little boys
At ball and bat and wild with noise
Is just as much a part of spring
As daffodils awakening.

Grace Tall

Fascination claims the heart,
A part of every springtime day,
Watching how the subtle way
Flowers lift green, hooded heads
Through darkened loam, through rain and sun,
Until the blossoms have begun,
Until the moment golden eyes
Meet the blue of April skies
And leave us breathless with surprise.

Pamela Vaull Starr

What Else but Spring?

A frisky colt, a fleecy lamb,
Blue sky from which warm sunshine spills,
Fat maple buds now blushing pink,
And yellow fields of daffodils.

D. A. Hoover

Easter Blessings

May you rejoice in the
Gladness of this
Easter season,
And may the message of
New life and hope
Remain with you always!

Pearl McKinney

April

April is a tease, a flirt,
swishing a breezy meadow-skirt,
twinkling a blink of changeful eye,
wearing a rainbow in her sky.

R. H. Grenville

Every blossom and flower
is an autograph of the Architect of the universe.

Author Unknown

A New Beginning

This newness,
this freshness, is all around.
This beauty
is bursting forth from the ground.
The singing
of birds flying by on wing,
the pure air of early spring,
symbols of
a new life, of one reborn
with spirit of Easter morn.

Mary Imogene Harris

Arrival of Spring

Now Spring in her grandeur is decking the hills,
And birds are rehearsing their lyrical trills.
The brooklets are singing like children at play
And welcoming Spring in her gala array.

Delphia Stubbs

Easter Gladness

With spring
Gladness will arrive.
Happy days will join
Easter fulfillment.
Faith will instill
Reverence.
The lily will grace
The power of His love;
His sunrise Resurrection
Brings peace.

Caroline S. Kotowicz

THE GOSPEL ACCORDING TO

ST. LUKE

The Real Story

On Easter Sunday, thousands of voices in sunrise services around the world will welcome Easter morning with the beloved hymn "The Old Rugged Cross."

The simple gospel song is not merely one favorite among many: in surveys it consistently rates as the hymn most Christians love best. Its message cuts across economic and language barriers. To the lonely, the friendless, the homesick, it has a special meaning.

Although the hymn is well known, the facts about its composition are less familiar. Few people recognize the name of its composer, George Bennard. Here is the story as it can best be pieced together.

George Bennard dropped out of school and became a coal miner at the age of fifteen. Later he was a Salvation Army drummer, then an evangelist preaching in every state except Utah and Louisiana. Although he composed more than 300 songs, he had no formal musical education.

His composing of "The Old Rugged Cross" was neither quick nor easy. In his lifetime it brought him little income and only small recognition. Born into poverty, he died in 1958 relatively unknown.

Several versions have been published about when, where, and how he composed "The Old Rugged Cross." Bennard said he had the melody and theme for some time before "finding the right words."

Interviewed in 1972, his eighty-two-year-old widow said, "He started it in 1912 (when he was thirty-nine) but polished it up over the next year or two. He came up with the complete version in the kitchen of our home in Albion, Michigan, singing it along with his guitar."

The last three verses, however, were not written there. In 1958 Bennard wrote to the Albion Historical Society explaining that the song was not composed entirely while he was in Albion. Because of his almost constant traveling, perhaps he did not remember all the towns where he worked on the song. He mentioned working on it in New York State. The Albion homesite has been officially recognized as the song's birthplace by the Michigan Historical Society.

For this itinerant soul saver and sacred poet, one of his greatest thrills was riding on "The Old Rugged Cross" float in the 1953 Rose Parade in Pasadena, California. Near the front was a flower-covered organ on which he played his famous song for the largest live audience of his lifetime. Another thrill came in 1954 when the Chamber of Commerce erected a twenty-foot rough-hewn cross near his Reed City, Michigan, home.

The composer died on October 10, 1958, at the age of eighty-five. Many recalled George Bennard's delightful sense of humor and his twinkling blue eyes. He was unselfish of his time and energy, as enthusiastic when his audience was small as when it was large.

In 1976 George Bennard was named a member of the Gospel Music Hall of Fame.

He often said he preferred to be remembered as a minister of the Gospel rather than a composer. "Hymn writing is just a runner-up," he said. No sermon he preached, however, exerted such far-reaching influence as "The Old Rugged Cross." It is his finest sermon, his greatest memorial.

C. D. Davenport

The Old Rugged Cross

Rev. George Bennard 1873–

George Bennard

On a hill far a-way stood an old rug-ged cross, The-

em-blem of suf-f'ring and shame; And I love that old cross where the

dear-est and best For a world of lost sin-ners was slain.

Chorus

So I'll cher-ish the old rug-ged cross, ___ Till my tro-phies at last I lay down; I will

cling to the old rug-ged cross, ___ And ex-change it some day for a crown.

Oh, that old rugged cross, so despised
by the world
Has a wondrous attraction to me;
For the dear Lamb of God left
His glory above
To bear it to dark Calvary.

In the old rugged cross, stained
with blood so divine,
A wondrous beauty I see;
For 'twas on that old cross Jesus
suffered and died.
To pardon and sanctify me.

To the old rugged cross
I will ever be true,
It's shame and reproach gladly bear;
Then He'll call me some day to
my home far away,
Where His glory forever I'll share.

I Have Found a Joy

I have heard a song
That set my heart to wandering.
    A cardinal sings
    Of nests and things.
Once more I am a child in spring.

I have seen a church,
Not one revered by poets' rhymes,
    But small and white.
    One April night
I heard the sound of vesper chimes.

I have worked for pay
For chores that seemed like play to me;
    For someone cared,
    And others shared.
That spring I would have worked for free.

I have known a child
Who smiled and secret thoughts expressed
    Of lambs and things
    That April brings.
I have known a child and I am blessed.

I have found a joy
Discovered on a hill in spring:
    God's love is near
    Throughout the year.
My faith grows strong remembering.

Alice Leedy Mason

Easter Is

Easter is a sunny time
When soft, warm breezes blow,
When crocus and bright daffodil
Replace the ice and snow.

Easter is a happy time
When birdsongs fill the air,
When childish laughter, light and gay,
Is ringing everywhere.

Easter is a joyous time,
So let your voice be heard
In joyful alleluias
To Christ, the Risen Lord.

Easter's Resurrection time,
And let us not forget
That He who rose up from the grave
Is living with us yet.

Easter is so many things,
All lovely to behold,
To cherish in fond memory,
To guard, and to enfold.

Mrs. Paul E. King

The Joys of Easter

Marshmallow eggs
And jelly beans,
A friendly Easter bunny,
Ribboned baskets,
Flower bonnets,
A day so bright and sunny,
Pink plush rabbits,
Yellow ducks,
Easter lilies fair,
Hyacinths, tulips
Blooming everywhere—
The earth is rain washed,
Born again;
The lark and robin sing,
And, Blessed Lord,
We thank You for
The joys that Easter brings.

Violet Bigelow Rourke

Some Thoughts at Easter Time

This is the season of the year that inspired Shakespeare in his *Romeo and Juliet* to pen the words "when well-apparelled April on the heel of limping winter treads." It is also a part of the calendar when the Christian Church holds one of its great festivals, Easter, to celebrate the Resurrection of Christ from the dead. A reminder, too, to all of us that dread winter has at last departed and that we can welcome lovely April in her prime. A time when man and beast, plants and flowers, birds and bees take a new lease on life.

It is also the time when fond parents and grandparents can gain pleasure from seeing the eyes of a child sparkle with delight when he or she receives the traditional gift of an Easter egg, be it hand painted in gay, exciting colors or a supreme, but short-lived, example of the art of the confectioner. A time for a rerun on TV of that splendid 1948 movie *Easter Parade* with Fred Astaire of the twinkling feet and lovely Judy Garland reminding us once again to put on an Easter bonnet and join the Easter Parade. And in small towns and villages everywhere, people will be doing just that—enjoying the Easter activities and the company of friends, a tradition which stretches back into the past. For it is the past which shapes our present and the future, which is yet to be.

I am reminded of an Easter Sunday back in 1722 when a Dutchman named Roggeween discovered an island lying in complete solitude in the vast South Pacific. He called it Easter Island to commemorate the day when he first set foot on that lonely outpost of civilization. It is difficult to understand what could have been the feeling, the astonishment, and the wonder of Roggeween and his companions when they saw white-skinned people among those who came down to the shore to meet them and when they discovered that those people were the guardians of a fantastic collection of immense statues carved of stone, some as high as a three-story building. The stone had been taken from the crater of an extinct volcano in the center of the island and carved into the finished colossi which were hauled and erected with infinite patience on platforms around the island. Statues with huge heads and pointed beards, with white men's features and, in many cases, with a giant block of red stone on top, looking as if some huge wig had been added for adornment, seemed to brood over the secrets of centuries long gone. Roggeween, on that Easter Sunday morning, must have offered up a prayer of thanksgiving for the wonder of such discoveries.

Easter reminds me, too, of the wealth of music which is part of this great season. The great anthems and cantatas, Johann Sebastian Bach's *Easter Oratorio*, the Easter Hymn from Mascagni's opera "Cavalleria Rusticana," and a host of other pieces, classical to popular.

For, above all, this is a happy time of the year. After the sorrows of Good Friday, Easter week represents a rebirth of the spirit, a reawakening of the joyous sights and sounds as winter moves forward into spring, a time for us to take stock of the present and to look forward to the lazy days of summer yet to come.

For the Christian, at this emotive period of the year, there is no doubt. He can well echo the words of G. K. Chesterton, that great man of English letters, "The Christian ideal has not been tried and found wanting; it has been found difficult and left untried."

Richard Thomas

Spring Bouquet

I went into
The woods today
And picked myself
A spring bouquet.
I found great beauty
In crannied nook
And flowers that bordered
Our gurgling brook.
Some flowers grew hidden
In secret places
With lovely colors
And upturned faces.

God has a meaning
In even the flower
If we just stop
And take one hour
And go upon
This pleasant quest
In search of peace
And happiness.
When you feel weary
Along life's way,
Just stop and pick
A spring bouquet.

Grace B. Rosser

In traditional Polish families, Easter Sunday is a day of feasting and celebration, and an occasion when "food is the main event," according to our friend Gail Rosinski. Unlike Christmas which is primarily a family holiday, Easter for the Poles is a time of generous hospitality, of open houses when friends and neighbors are welcomed with a lavish buffet of delicious Polish delicacies.

Because many Polish people are devout Catholics, much of the Easter holiday is highlighted by religious traditions and symbols. After observing the forty-day Lenten fast by eating little or no meat, the Polish people approach the Easter feast with unbridled enthusiasm.

The Rosinski family observes the tradition of preparing hard-cooked eggs on Good Friday night. There are two kinds of Easter eggs—those dyed a solid color, the *krashanky*, and the exquisitely patterned *pysanky*, which are true folk art.

There are several legends surrounding Easter eggs, both in Poland and the Ukraine. One story tells us that Mary Magdalene and her friends went to the tomb of Jesus to anoint His body with fragrant spices, carrying a basket of food with them for their lunch. When they had completed their sad task, the legend says, the women sat down to eat and discovered that the hard-cooked eggs had taken on every color of the rainbow. Another story suggests that red-colored eggs are symbolic of the blood that was shed by Jesus on the cross.

To create the lovely pysanky, the egg is blown out, and the shell is patiently and artistically decorated by means of a special stylus dipped in beeswax. The pysanky may be decorated with liturgical symbols such as the lamb and the cross, with flowers to represent love and charity, with roosters for the fulfillment of wishes, or with geometric designs of all kinds.

In the Rosinski household, "Grandma prepares a special egg which is hard-cooked and then peeled. She decorates it with fresh, whole cloves in the shape of a cross and places it in the basket of food that will be blessed at church on Holy Saturday," Gail said.

The children in the family prepare the baskets,

KIELBASA

1½ pounds lean boneless pork
½ pound boneless veal
1 teaspoon salt
¼ teaspoon pepper
1 clove garlic, crushed
1 tablespoon mustard seed
¼ cup crushed ice
½ teaspoon margarine
   Sausage casings

Cut meat into small chunks. Grind with seasonings and ice; add margarine and mix well. Stuff into casings. Place sausages in large pot and cover with cold water; bring to a boil and boil for 15 minutes. Simmer for 2 hours.

Polish Easter

and the youngest has the honor of carrying the basket up to the priest for his blessing. All sorts of foods go into the basket: salt to symbolize "the salt of the earth," eggs to symbolize new life, and a butter lamb or lamb cake decorated with a small Polish flag to indicate victory over death and also to represent Christ as the Paschal Lamb. Many families add specially baked breads, and most include several links of homemade *kielbasa*, the spicy Polish sausage.

After the baskets are blessed, the family returns home to begin the elaborate preparations for Easter Sunday, when the feasting starts at breakfast. In many Polish homes, the father slices an Easter egg and distributes a piece to each family member as a wish for happiness in the coming year.

"Polish people take great pride in the way the table is set for Easter Sunday," Gail said. "We always use our finest linen and silver, and traditionally the centerpiece is a bouquet of pussy willows to symbolize the rebirth of spring and the rebirth of Christians who celebrate Christ's Resurrection."

Friends, neighbors, relatives—absolutely everyone is welcome to the sumptuous Easter buffet, and the mother and father greet each guest at the door with a slice of hard-cooked egg, again signifying the family's wish that each guest will have good health, good luck, and happiness.

The Easter buffet table is laden with foods of every kind—"so much that it's hard to find room for it all," Gail said. There is borscht, the clear soup; homemade kielbasa; red beets with horseradish sauce. "Beets are a very common vegetable in Poland," Gail pointed out, "and the horseradish sauce has vinegar in it which represents the bitter vinegar that Christ was given to drink when He asked for water from the cross."

The Polish Easter buffet also features a vast selection of hot and cold meats: lamb, pork, ham, beef, turkey, goose, roast pork, and steaming links of kielbasa. Desserts are also plentiful; there's Grandmother's cheesecake with raisins, *cruschiki* or Polish love knots, and the moist *babka* which resembles a fruitcake.

Bea Bourgeois

CWIKLA (Red Beets)

3 cups cooked or canned beets, drained and coarsely chopped
6 ounces cream-style horseradish
1 tablespoon brown sugar
1 teaspoon vinegar
¼ teaspoon salt

Combine all ingredients. Cover and refrigerate for 3 days.

Spring Flowers

Spring flowers
Always come as a surprise,
A blessed treat
For winter-weary eyes.
You had forgotten
Just how fresh and bright
A daffodil could be
Or how the light
Seemed to be
Prisoned in a tulip's cup,
Like tiny
Goblets lifted up.

Edna Jaques

Promise

Little crocus, shivering there
In the windy, misty air,
Forecasting lovely, lilting spring,
Renewing hope in everything,
You have helped my heart to sing.

Spring brings roses, lilacs, too,
Violets, pansies fresh as dew;
But if I named a favorite flower
In garden bed or woodland bower,
You would be first—queen of this hour!

Lillie D. Chaffin

The Warmth of Spring

Little colts caper and kick up their heels.
They race toward their mothers when ready for meals.

Wobbly-kneed calves stand close to the barn
Out of the wind where it's sheltered and warm.

Woolly lambs, all of them, know right away
That the first thing to do is to learn how to play.

New kittens are mewing; new mice try to squeak;
New birds in their nests will fly in a week.

In spring, in warm weather, all over our farm,
There's hardly a baby that hasn't been born.

                                        Dorothy Aldis

Easter and Spring

Easter and spring come almost hand in hand, offering an appropriate ritual for both the observance of the Resurrection and the arrival of spring. The risen Christ brought great joy to His people on the day of His Resurrection. And spring, a new season of birth, of hope and faith, brings joy to mankind.

Year after year, each season in turn assumes its role in the calendar of time. Spring, with its songs and flutes, buds and blossoms, brings cheer and strength and hope and the solace of faith.

That first spring blossom is as glorious to the eye as is the meaning of the Resurrection to the heart and soul of man. Humanity cannot ignore the greatness of all things in nature and life and cannot ignore that behind the great changes in the seasons and behind all life is the work, labor, and love of the Master of all.

One cannot close his eyes to the spring beauty that unfolds around him: the new green, the flowers, the longer days of sun, the warming land, the budding trees and plants. He cannot close his ears to the birdsongs that resound from orchard and woodland, from dooryard and pasture, from field and fen.

Nor can he close his ears and his heart to the glorious message of Easter as expressed in the hymns and from the pulpits of churches across the land. Each person becomes aware that there is something far greater than the accumulation of wealth and material things. He learns that all riches must be in faith and spirit and love. And with these truths before him, there will no longer be room in his heart for greed and hate. There will be room only for love and compassion, room only for peace and the richness of its content.

Lansing Christman

Vernal Spring

H. G. Adams

A bursting into greenness,
A waking as from sleep,
A twitter and a warble
That make the pulses leap,
A watching as in childhood
For the flowers that, one by one,
Open their golden petals
To woo the fitful sun.
A gust, a flash, a gurgle,
A wish to shout and sing,
As, filled with hope and gladness,
We have the vernal spring.

Definition

Edith Shaw Butler

How can one define the spring?
The time of earth's awakening,
The time when bulb and seed and root
Thrust up the new and tender shoot,

The song of birds—all this is part
Of wonderment that fills the heart.
Define it thus—a child's blond head
Bent eagerly over a flower bed.

April

It's lemonade, it's lemonade, it's daisy.
It's a roller-skating, scissor-grinding day;
It's gingham-waisted, chocolate flavored, lazy,
With the children flower-scattered at their play.

It's the sun like watermelon,
And the sidewalks overlaid
With a glaze of yellow yellow
Like a jar of marmalade.

It's the mower gently mowing,
And the stars like startled glass,
While the mower keeps on going
Through a waterfall of grass,

Then the rich magenta evening
Like a sauce upon the walk,
And the porches softly swinging
With a hammockful of talk.

It's the hobo at the corner
With his lilac-sniffing gait,
And the shy departing thunder
Of the fast departing skate.

It's lemonade, it's lemonade, it's April!
A water sprinkler, puddle winking time,
When a boy who peddles slowly,
   with a smile remote and holy,
Sells you April chocolate flavored for a dime.

Marcia Lee Masters

Our shut-in days are over!
 The grass is turning green;
And here and there, along the roads,
 Wildflowers can be seen.
The valleys' last small patches
 Of snow have given up
To be replaced by lacy fern
 And fragile buttercup.

In all the wooded areas,
 The trees are budding out;
The mystifying beauties
 Of spring are all about.
For young and old alike, it means
 Vacation time is here—
The time we all look forward to
 The rest of every year.

Though we find winter lovely
 With its quiet, mellow days,
When springtime rolls around again,
 Our hearts are glad always.
With hours that are made golden
 By its pleasant warmth of sun,
It is the gateway season
 To our days of outdoor fun.

Nadine Brothers Lybarger

The Gateway Season

ACKNOWLEDGMENTS

COLOR ART AND PHOTO CREDITS
(in order of appearance)

Front and back cover, Alpha Photo Associates; inside front cover, Gerald Koser; "Azalea Trail" in Callaway Gardens along Mockingbird Lake near Pine Mountain, Georgia, Ken Dequaine; Nest among blossoms, H. Armstrong Roberts; Springtime on the farm, Gerald Koser; Spring greenhouse, Alpha Photo Associates; Pear blossoms framing Hood River Valley and Mount Hood, Oregon, William D. McKinney; Oregon Pipe Cactus National Monument, Alpha Photo Associates; Tulip beds, Fred Sieb; Colorful pathway, Harold M. Lambert; Aisles of daffodils, Fred Sieb; Spring bouquet, Colour Library International (USA) Limited; Harbinger of spring, Colour Library International (USA) Limited; THIS IS MY BODY, THE LAST SUPPER, Robert Heuel, Gerald Koser; EASTER MORNING, Robert Heuel, Gerald Koser; Seagulls at sunset, Robert Taylor; Easter glow, Fred Sieb; Easter and spring, Fred Sieb; Crocus bed, Colour Library International (USA) Limited; Horses grazing in spring pasture, Gottlieb Hampfler; Springtime smile, Robert Taylor; Garden blossoms, Alpha Photo Associates; Springtime reflection, Colour Library International (USA) Limited; Meandering streams, Freelance Photographers Guild; inside back cover, Gerald Koser.

APRIL by R. H. Grenville, Originally published by CAPPER'S WEEKLY. PUSSY WILLOWS by Arthur Guiterman. From DEATH AND GENERAL PUTNAM AND 101 OTHER POEMS by Arthur Guiterman. Copyright 1935 by E. P. Dutton & Co., Inc. Renewal © 1963 by Mrs. Vida Lindo Guiterman. SPRINGTIME IN THE DESERT by Sudie Stuart Hager. From EARTH-BOUND by Sudie Stuart Hager, Copyright © by Sudie Stuart Hager. SPRINGTIME ON THE FARM by Eunice Elmore Heizer. From ECHOES by Eunice Elmore Heizer, Copyright © 1967 by Eunice Elmore Heizer. Published by Dorrance & Company. THE ANGEL, SPRING by Ruby Davenport Kish. From A TOUCH OF TIME by Ruby Davenport Kish, Copyright © 1977 by Ruby Davenport Kish, Published by Dorrance & Company. BUDS OF BEAUTY (originally titled FLOWERS) by Mabelle A. Lyon. Previously published in PRAIRIE POET. MARCH WINDS by Essie L. Mariner. From her book ENCOUNTERED. APRIL by Marcie Lee Masters. From CONTEMPORARY POETRY (Winter 1944). Also reprinted in the author's book IN-TENT ON EARTH. Reprinted by permission of the author. MAUNDY THURSDAY by Alice Kennelly Roberts. Copyrighted. used with permission of the author. EASTER and RESUR-RECTION DAY (originally titled SPRING) by Leon Eugene Wright. From COME SHARE WITH US by Leon Eugene Wright, Copyright © 1959 by Dorrance & Company. Our sincere thanks to the following author whose address we were unable to locate: H. G. Adams for VERNAL SPRING.

Join us in a special tribute . . .

Mother's Day Ideals is a glorious tapestry praising the attributes of Motherhood and the beauty of springtime.

Enjoy a special poem for Mother, entitled "A Daughter Remembers"; learn how to enhance your garden with a colorful variety of spring flowers; and choose from delightful spring activities the whole family can enjoy. Beautiful color photography illustrates this enchanting volume.

A gift subscription is the perfect way to say "Happy Mother's Day" all year round! Subscribe for yourself, too, and enjoy the beautiful world of Ideals!